T0086358

SHOUT HALLELUJAH!

At Home Solo-Quarantine
COVID-19 Global Pandemic
Challenges Tests for the Elderly
-Spiritual, Mental and Physical
#50/50/50

SHARON HUNT

SHOUT HALLELUJAH!
AT HOME SOLO-QUARANTINE COVID-19 GLOBAL PANDEMIC CHALLENGES TESTS FOR THE ELDERLY -SPIRITUAL, MENTAL AND PHYSICAL #50/50/50

The work has been developed by the author. The author is not a psychologist. The suggested challenges are for entertainment only. Safety is of upmost.

iUniverse books may be ordered through booksellers or by contacting:

iUniverse
1663 Liberty Drive
Bloomington, IN 47403
www.iuniverse.com
844-349-9409

ISBN: 978-1-6632-2121-6 (sc)
ISBN: 978-1-6632-2122-3 (e)

Library of Congress Control Number: 2021907437

Print information available on the last page.

iUniverse rev. date: 04/15/2021

Thank You for buying this book. Challenge yourself daily. Have a good time and a good life. God Bless You!

Sincerely
Sharon Hunt, Author

CONTENTS

DEDICATION

The author dedicates all of her work to Jesus Christ, who is the head of her life. He gives her all ideas for her work and anoints her books. She always uses the following scripture:

> "Commit thy works unto the Lord, and thy thought shall be established."
>
> PROVERBS 16:3

Also, this book is dedicated to all elderly, who live alone and are going through solo quarantine indoors. The author has given the term solo-quarantine to the elderly who do not go outside during quarantine. Therefore, the author has put together her version of challenges tests that maybe practiced over a 50-day quarantine period.

AFTER COMPLETION OF THE DAY'S CHALLENGE -THE PERSON SHOULD- SHOUT OUTLOUD – 'HALLELUJAH!'

PREFACE

The purpose is to motivate the elderly people, living along, in three ways each day- spiritually, mentally and physically. The elderly, who are physically able, are encouraged to set aside 50 minutes each day and try one of the challenges each day for 50 minutes.

There are three main objectives in the solo -quarantine book:

1. Give daily positive words to concentrate on to bring peace and gratitude experiences that may be obtained through various challenges,
2. Suggest to people who are living alone how to engage in solo-quarantine experiences,
3. Set a maximum time limit of 50 minutes to achieve all three challenges for that day.

A timer should be set for 10 minutes for Spiritual and 40 minutes for the combined achievement of mental and physical health challenges.

Each challenge is three dimensional – spiritual, mental and physical. Hopefully, participation in the daily challenges will contribute to a daily good -quality of well- being. One should work on the each challenge until it is achieved in the allotted 50 minutes time period or Continue to work until reaching the time goals.

INTRODUCTION

Due to the global coronavirus-19 pandemic, many elderly have decided to stay indoors rather than go outside. Some of these people are prohibited to go outdoors or have limited exposure to out doors or visit other people.

Often times, the "new normal" may cause these people to slowly slip into despair. Therefore, this project has been prepared as a friendly easy-tool to help the solo-quarantine individuals to get involved in daily 50 minute long – challenges, which may promote spiritual renewal, mental rejuvenation and physical motion, although low impact.

All of the challenges involved tests that contribute to the well-being, while solo-quarantining with self-directed challenges. (No one should be present to interfere with progress.) The meaning of - #50/50/50= Fifty days of challenges, Fifty different topics and Fifty minutes to complete each day's challenges.

In this section, the author will explain her Past experiences of working with elderly, fifty feel good words assigned to the fifty -three-dimensional challenges, and what the elderly needs to do to get involved in each challenge.

Author's Career with the Rural Elderly Research

In her work career, the author was on a research team that covered ten states seeking to find out the quality of well-being of the Rural elderly. The research was funded by the United Department of Agriculture (USDA).

The research was done on elderly living in Alabama, Arkansas, Missouri, Mississippi, South Carolina, Tennessee, Texas, Georgia,

Maryland and Virginia. The research covered asking elderly about their quality of well-being, economic, independence, economic well-being (perception financial/income adequacy), independence(freedom from physical, social and/ or economic constraints), psychological/life satisfaction (control, optimism, enjoyment), happiness with life, satisfaction, and social relations(level of social involvement), expectations for activity, consistency in activities over time, satisfaction with socially-related activities, such as, religious organizations.

Daily Activities

However, this book is the author's version of solo-quarantine challenges.

There is a feel -good word of the day to assist in Achieving positive outcomes. The daily feel good word is the author's selection of a coping mechanism for the solo-quarantine experience.

Thc idea is to combine a daily feel- good word or well -being word suggested to celebrate positive outcome feelings as a result of meditating on spiritual happenings in the Holy Bible (King James Version) and achieving the remaining two challenges. The author believes in the biblical scripture- In everything give thanks for this is the will of God in Christ Jesus concerning you. I Thessalonians 5:18

In the meditation, the person should meditate on ten (10) things that will give you a happy and love connected feeling. Each day after the person completes the three dimensional challenges, spiritual, mental and physical (SMP) the person should be rejuvenated the whole day.

The spiritual, mental and physical health experiences are to be completed in 50 minutes to give a wonderful outcome and feel good at the end of the day.

Goal I: Spiritual Health -Gain Peace and Gratitude To generate a peaceful outcome, the author has developed each spiritual experience activity centered around a biblical story and a positive word for each person meditate on for 10 minute

The person is to meditate on how to Find happiness and love in each experience.

The timer is to be set for 10 minutes for meditation to find happiness and love in the biblical experience and positive word.

Goal II. Mental Health- Stimulate the Brain Cells

To get the person thinking while exercising, the author has selected easy memories for each person to recite. The mental challenges is to count out loud the suggested activity while performing the physical challenge. As a choice, favorite music maybe played in the background as one recites out loud the mental activity.

Goal III. Physical Health Challenge- Get the Body in Motion To get the person in motion, simple physical challenges with low impact, however, simple with out the purchase of exercise equipment.

Check with your doctor before beginning the exercise program. Bad signs that tell you are exercising too hard to include gasping for breath, nausea, extreme tiredness or exhaustion, joint pain and muscle soreness, that lasts longer than a day. If you get any of these signs you should rest and start again at a slower pace.

You should talk to a doctor if you detect an irregular heart rate, a rapid drop in your heart rate during exercise. If you have

Sudden confusion, pressure in the center of your chest or in your throat or incoordination, cold sweats, blueness or fainting check with your doctor. Do what is right for you.

Chapters Design

All chapters are designed in the same way. First there is a feel- good word to name each chapter

And introduction to the chapter. There should be two Pages to each chapter.

Part I

Spiritual Health Meditation

Experience

Happy and Love Connected Challenges

(Biblical scriptures from the King James' Version of The Holy Bible.)

Maximum Time Limit: 10 minutes

Part II
Mental Health Challenge Recitation Experience

Maximum Time Limit:40 minutes

Part III
Physical Health Exercise
Challenge Experience Maximum Time Limit: 40 minutes

On the second page of each day, a list of hints is included.

The Spiritual Health Happy and Love Challenge-

The challenge has a 10 minute meditation experience to get the mind to have a final outcome set to bring a happy and love experience that results in total peace.

Limit meditation time to 10 minutes.

Immediately, reset the timer for 40 minutes and complete the combined mental health and physical Health challenges.

The Mental Health Challenge is 40 minutes. The challenge is a recitation experience. The person is asked to recite out loud assigned activities while they are completing the physical health challenge.

The author has provided a page of hints for several Mental challenges or the person may develop their Own challenges.

A person may choose to play a choice of background music. The music may assist the brain in remembering Answers.

The Physical Health Challenge is to engage in a low impact exercise. Each exercise has been given a fun name by the author.

For example – exercises for arms – 'duck quacks' with arms, 'race horse' leg kicks, 'pony' knee lifts, etc.

Things You will Need:

1. Room indoors – Prepare a space in a room that is safe, properly ventilated and lighted. Make the area clean. Free from animals.
2. Straight Back Chair – Use a straight back chair for some exercises.
3. Small Table- Use a small table for holding props, such as water, towels, etc.

4. Small Rug or Floor Mat – Use the small rug or floor mat for floor exercises.
5. Holy Bible – Determine your method of meditating And refer to the Holy Bible for Scriptures.
6. Telephone -Keep nearby if need assistance during a fall or other emergency.
7. Timer - Keep a portable timer or a ticking clock with an alarm to with each day in the challenges.
8. Water- Keep a bottle of water nearby, drink plenty of fluids, Especially during the warm weather. Do not drink sodas.
9. Clothing and Shoes – Wear comfortable clothes and safe good shoes and socks.
10. Time of Day – Your choice-Try to spend at least 50 minutes each day.

Fifty (50) Days of Challenges
In
Fifty(50) Chapters

CHAPTER 1

FEEL -GOOD WORD OF THE DAY: OBEDIENCE

On the first day of the Solo-Quarantine Experience -Celebrate Obedience

Def as compliance with an order, request or law or submission to another's authority

Goal I: Gain peace and gratitude

Part I -Spiritual Health -Happy and Love Connected Challenge

Meditate for 10 minutes on how you can be happy and experience love at the end of meditating on the positive side of obedience and the 'Nineveh Experience'.

Part II Mediation Experience

Take steps to read the story and think about the

"Ninevah" Experience -Obedience.

Short Story on Jonah.

Jonah's failure to obey lead to major problems. However, when he obeyed and preached Ninevah -The people were happy and loved God and Jonah went to save the people.......(see scripture)

Meditate on 10 feelings of happiness and lovingly things as a result of learning of Jonah's Obedience.

Goal II: Stimulate Brain Cells

Part I -Mental Health Challenge – Maximum Time Limit 40 minutes (both mental and physical health challenges are done together)

To recite a given task within the time limit while completing the physical health challenge.

Part II – Recitation Experience

Recite the names of 100 people you know and identify why you love them. See many types of love.

The idea is to focus on the matter at hand.

Goal III: Get the Body in Motion

Part I-Physical Health Challenge -Maximum Time Limit 40 minutes (recite mental health activity as you do physical challenge).

Part II Exercise Activity

'Kangaroo Boxing' -Make 100 simulate shadow boxing strokes within 40 minutes while reciting mental exercise.

SHOUT HALLELUJAH!

Biblical Scriptures

> And the Lord spake unto the fish, and it vomited out Jonah upon the dry land.
>
> JONAH 2:10

> And the word of the Lord, came unto Jonah the second time saying,
>
> JONAH 3:1

> "Arise, go unto Ninevah that great city, and preach unto it the preaching that I bid thee.
>
> JONAH 3:2

Hints: Love in the 'Ninevah' Experience

Types of Love

There are six basic types of love:

1. Agape -Altruistic love-loves just because
2. Eros -Romantic love -maybe passionate love
3. Storge- Friendship love -begins as friends
4. Pragma -Practical love – mutual love
5. Ludis -Playful love -loves but no commitment
6. Mania love- Obsessive love

CHAPTER 2

FEEL- GOOD WORD OF THE DAY: COMMITMENT

On the Second Day(2) of the Solo-Quarantine Experience -Celebrate Commitment

Def the state or quality of being dedicated to a cause, activity

Goal I: Gain Peace and Gratitude

Part I Spiritual Health Happy and Love Challenge
10 minutes

Part II Meditation Experience

Meditate on 10 commitments in Happy and Love you give similar to what Mary showed in her commitment to God in the birth of a Saviour, Jesus.

Take steps to meditate on the 'Salvation Experience'.

Biblical Scripture

> And he sent them to Bethlehem and said, Go and search diligently for the young child; and when ye have found him, bring me word again, that I may come and worship him also.
>
> MATTHEW 2:8

Goal 2: Stimulate the Brain Cells

Part 1. Mental Health Challenge
40 minutes time challenge

Part 2. Mental Health Activity
Name 50 ethnic groups in the United States
(See Hints)

Goal 3: Get the Body in Motion

Part 1 Physical Health Challenge
40 minutes time limit

Part 2 Exercise Activity
Jumping Jack Rabbits -Make 100 Jumping Jacks

SHOUT HALLELUJAH!

Hints:
Samples of Ethnic Groups in United States

1. English
2. Germans
3. Italians
4. Irishmen
5. French
6. Mexicans

7. African-Americans
8. Jamaicans
9. Nigerians
10. Jewish
11. Bahamians
12. Haitians
13. Australians
14. Scottish
15. Hindus
16. Cambodians
17. Thias from Thailand
18. Vietnamese
19. Chinese
20. Japanese
21. Canadians
22. El Salvadorians
23. Congolese
24. Cubans
25. Nicaraguans
26. Cherokees
27. Creeks
28. Chickasaws
29. Seminoles
30. Choctaws
31. Samoans
32. Greeks
33. Laotians
34. Arabians
35. Ethiopians
36. Sioux
37. Sac and Fox
38. Black Foot
39. Puerto Ricans
40. Dominicans
41. Peruvians
42. Czechs

43. Slovenians
44. Russians
45. Canadians
46. Utes
47. Ugandans
48. Palestine's
49. Moroccans
50. Taiwanese

CHAPTER 3

FEEL- GOOD WORD OF THE DAY: FREEDOM

On the Third Day (3) of the Solo-Quarantine Experience -Freedom
Def is having the ability to act or change without constraint.

Goal I. Gain Peace and Gratitude

Part 1 Spiritual Health Happy and Love Connected Challenge
10 minutes

Part 2 Meditation Experience
Freedom – Achieving freedom in Jabez prayer
Find 10 ways you can find happiness and love from meditating on Jabez's Prayer.
The 'Jabez's Experience'

Biblical Scripture

> And Jabez called on the God of Israel, saying oh that -thou wouldest bless me indeed, and enlarge my coast, and that thine hand might be with me, and that thou wouldest keep me from evil, that it may not grieve me!
>
> And God granted him that which he requested."
>
> I CHRONICLES 4:10

Goal 2: Stimulate the Brain Cells

Part 1 -Mental Health Challenge
40 minutes

Part 2 –Recitation Experience
Recite in alphabetical order, the names of 50 U. S. States.
(See Hints)

Goal III: Get the Body in Motion

Part I Physical Health Challenge
40 minutes

Part 2 Exercise Activity
Spending Wheel -'Run -in Place' for 40 minutes
SHOUT HALLELUJAH!

Hint- List of 50 United States

1. Alabama
2. Alaska
3. Arizona
4. Arkansas
5. California
6. Colorado

7. Connecticut
8. Delaware
9. Florida
10. Georgia
11. Hawaii
12. Idaho
13. Illinois
14. Indiana
15. Iowa
16. Kansas
17. Kentucky
18. Louisiana
19. Maine
20. Maryland
21. Massachusetts
22. Michigan
23. Minnesota
24. Mississippi
25. Missouri
26. Montana
27. Nebraska
28. Nevada
29. New Hampshire
30. New Jersey
31. New Mexico
32. New York
33. North Carolina
34. North Dakota
35. Ohio
36. Oklahoma
37. Oregon
38. Pennsylvania
39. Rhode Island
40. South Carolina
41. South Dakota
42. Tennessee

43. Texas
44. Utah
45. Vermont
46. Virginia
47. Washington
48. West Virginia
49. Wisconsin
50. Wyoming

CHAPTER 4

FEEL -GOOD WORD OF THE DAY: GREATEST LOVE

On the Fourth Day(4) of the Solo-Quarantine Experience -Celebrate - Greatest Love

Def an intense feeling without constraints

Goal 1: Gain Peace and Gratitude

Part 1 Spiritual Health Happy and love Challenge
10 minutes

Part 2 Mediation Experience
Meditate 10 types of Greatest Love to give to people you love.
'Galilee Sea Experience'
Love One Another

Biblical Scriptures

> 10 Then the eleven disciples went away into Galilee into a mountain where Jesus had appointed them

19 Go ye therefore and teach all nations baptizing them in the name of the Father, and of the Son, and of the Holy Ghost:

20 Teaching them to observe all things, whatsoever I have commanded you: and, lo, I am with you always, even unto the end of the world. Amen

MATTHEW 28:10, 19,20

Goal 2: Stimulate the Brain Cells

Part 1 Mental Health Challenge
40 minutes

Part 2 Recite the alphabet twice forward and twice backwards while completing physical health challenge
Starting with A
Backwards -Start with Z

Goal 3: Get the Body in Motion

Part 1 Physical Health Challenge
40 minutes

Part 2 Exercise Activity
'Sumo Wrestler's Bow' -Stand up straight – ' Bow to the waist' 100 times

SHOUT HALLELUJAH!

CHAPTER 5

FEEL -GOOD WORD OF THE DAY: PATIENCE

On the Fifth Day(5) of the Solo-Quarantine Experience -Celebrate -Patience

Def the ability to remain calm when dealing with difficult or annoying situation, task, or person.

Goal I: Gain Peace and Gratitude

Part 1 Spiritual Health Happy and Love Connected Challenge
10 minutes

Part 2 Meditation Experience
Mount Caramel Experience
Compare your measure of patience as the Mount Caramel Experience.
Elijah showed patience in God's provision of water to the people.
Mount Caramel Experience

Biblical Scripture

> So Ahab went up to eat and to drink. And Elijah went up to the top of Carmel; and he can't himself down upon the earth, and put his face between his knees.
>
> I KINGS 18:42

Meditate 10 feelings of happiness and lovely ideas
After reading the scripture.

Goal II: Stimulate the Brain Cells

Part 1 Mental Health Challenge
40 minutes

Part 2 Recitation Experience
Recite the names of 50 largest cities in the United States
(See -Hints- Largest Cities)

Goal III: Get the Body in Motion

Part 1 Physical Health Challenge
40 minutes

Part 2 Exercise Activity
Step Ladder Simulation-
Simulate -Walking up and down the steps - 2 steps up and 2 steps down -50 times

SHOUT HALLELUJAH!

Hints: Hints largest cities in the U.S.

1. New York
2. Los Angeles
3. Chicago

4. Houston
5. Phoenix
6. Philadelphia
7. San Antonio
8. San Antonio
9. San Diego
10. Dallas
11. San Jose
12. Austin
13. Jacksonville
14. Fort Worth
15. Columbus
16. Charlotte
17. San Francisco
18. Indianapolis
19. Seattle
20. Denver
21. Boston
22. El Paso
23. Nashville
24. Detroit
25. Oklahoma City
26. Portland
27. Las Vegas
28. Memphis
29. Louisville
30. Baltimore

CHAPTER 6

FEEL -GOOD WORD OF THE DAY: CALM

On the Sixth (6) Day the Solo-Quarantine Experience -Celebrate- Calm
Def a period or condition of freedom from a rough situation

Goal I: Gain Peace and Gratitude

Part 1 Spiritual Health Happy and Love Connective
10 minutes

Part 2 Meditation Experience
'Upper Room Experience'-

Biblical Scriptures

18 Jesus gathered his disciples together for His last supper.

19 And he took bread; and gave thanks, and brake it, and gave unto them, saying, This is my body which is given for you: this do in remembrance of me.

> 20 Likewise, also the cup after supper, saying; This cup
> is the new testament in my blood, which is shed for you.
> Luke 22:18, 19, 20

Meditate on 10 methods to bring you calm,
Happiness and lovely feelings after studying about the last supper.

Goal II: Stimulate the Brain Cells

Part 1 Mental Health Challenge
40 minutes

Part 2 Recite the names of 25 types of wildflowers
(see Hints-Types of wildflowers)

Goal III: Get the Body in Motion

Part 1 Physical Health Challenge
40 minutes

Part 2 Exercise Activity
'Wrench Twist' -Twist from left to right -100 times

SHOUT HALLELUJAH!

(Hints: Names of wildflowers)

1. Daisy
2. Orchid
3. Tulip
4. Baby Blue
5. Gold Yarrow
6. Blanket Flower
7. Pussy Willow
8. Cherokee Rose Angel
9. Sweet Violet

10. Wind Flower
11. Cherokee Rose
12. Baby Blue Eyes
13. Barren Strawberry
14. Cornflower
15. Digitalis
16. Flickweed
17. Red Indian Paint
18. Alfalfa
19. Agave
20. Honey Bells
21. Wild Hyacinth
22. Red Clover
23. Large Hop Clover
24. Dandelion
25. Black Elderberry

CHAPTER 7

FEEL -GOOD WORD OF THE DAY: KINDNESS

On the Seventh (7) Day of the Solo-Quarantine Experience Celebrate - Kindness

Def is a type of behavior marked by acts of generosity, consideration or concern for others without expecting praise or reward.

Goal I: Gain Peace and Gratitude

Part 1 Spiritual Health Happy and Love Connected Challenge
10 minutes

Part 2 Meditation Experience
'Good Samaritan Experience'

Biblical Scriptures

33And a certain Samaritan as he journeyed came where
he was: and when he saw him, he had compassion on him

> 34 And went to him, and bound up his wound, pouring in oil and wine, and set him on his own beast, and brought him to an inn, and took care of him,
>
> 35 And on the morrow when he departed, he took out two pence, and gave them to the host, and said unto him, Take care of him; and And whatsoever then spendest more, which I come again, I will repay thee.
>
> LUKE 10:33- 35

Meditate on ten(10) happiness and love feelings as a result of kindness shown to you or you have shown kindness to others.

Goal II: Stimulate the Brain Cells

Part 1. Mental Health Challenge
40 minutes

Part 2. Give examples of 100 acts of kindness done by you in the last 5 years. (Personal, you write these.)

Goal III: Get the Body in Motion

Part 1. Physical Health Challenge
40 minutes

Part 2 Exercise Activity
'Wrestler's Move' Simulate -100 kickboxing motions-50 with right leg and 50 with the left leg.

SHOUT HALLELUJAH!

CHAPTER 8

FEEL- GOOD WORD OF THE DAY: FOOD

On the eighth(8) Day of the Solo-Quarantine Experience Celebrate -Food

Def food is any substance consumed to provide nutritional support of a person.

Goal I: Gain Peace and Gratitude

Part 1 Spiritual Health Happy and Love
Connected Challenge
10 minutes

Part 2 Meditation Experience – Positive food
From God

Biblical Scriptures

> 31 Therefore take no thought, saying, what shall we eat? Or, what shall we drink? Or, wherewithal shall we be clothed?

> 33 But seek ye first the kingdom of God, and his righteousness: and all these things shall be added unto you.
>
> 34 Take therefore no thought for the morrow: for the morrow shall take thought for the things of itself. Sufficient into the day in the evil thereof.
>
> MATTHEW 6:31, 33, 34

Meditate on 10 types of foods – soul or other types
That makes you happy and loving when you hear about them.

Goal II: Stimulate the Brain Cells

Part 1 Mental Health Challenge
40 minutes

Part 2 Recitation Experience
Name 25 types of cheeses
(See Hints)

Goal III: Get the Body in Motion

Part 1 Physical Health Challenge
40 minutes

Part 2 Exercise Activity
Windmills Windups -Make 100 windmill motions with both arms

SHOUT HALLELUJAH!

(Hints: Different types of cheese)

1. Cheddar
2. Swiss
3. Gouda
4. Blue

5. Cream cheese
6. Cottage cheese
7. Provolone Cheese
8. Mozzarella
9. Roquefort
10. Camembert
11. Queso Blanco
12. Brie
13. Neufchatel
14. Gorgonzola
15. Asiago
16. Stilton
17. Appenzeller
18. Raclette
19. Ricotta
20. Feta
21. Parmesan
22. Danish Blue
23. Grane Pademo
24. Quark
25. Hoop Cheese

CHAPTER 9

FEEL -GOOD WORD OF THE DAY: JOYFUL

On the Ninth (9) Day of Solo-Quarantine Experience -Celebrate Joyful
Def feeling expressing or causing great pleasure and happiness

Goal I: Gain Peace and Gratitude

Part 1 Spiritual Health Happy and Love Connected Challenge
10 minutes

Part 2 Meditation Experience
Meditate on Psalm 100
'Songs of Praise Experience'
A Psalm of Praise

Biblical Scripture

1 Make a joyful noise unto the LORD, all ye lands.

2 Serve the LORD with gladness: come before his presence
with singing

3 Know ye that the LORD he is God It is he that hath made us, and not we ourselves: we are this people, and the sheep of his pasture.

4 Enter into his gates with thanksgiving, and into his courts with praise: be thankful unto him, and bless his name.

5 For the LORD is good: his mercy is everlasting: and his truth endured to all generations.

PSALM 100:1-5

Meditate on 10 songs that make you happy and in love.

Goal II: Stimulate the Brain Cells

Part 1 Mental Health Challenge
40 minutes

Part 2 Sing 1 each
Patriotic Song, Christmas Song, kid's song, love song or hymn -Within allotted time limit
(See Hints for song)

Goal III: Get the Body in Motion

Part 1. Physical Health Challenge
40 minutes

Part 2. Exercise Activity
'Down Hill Snow Skiing' -Simulate -100 'Snow -Skiing' motions by sliding from side to side.

SHOUT HALLELUJAH!

(Hint – eg. Patriotic Songs-
National Anthem and Negro National Anthem)

CHAPTER 10

FEEL -GOOD WORD OF THE DAY: THANKFULNESS

On the tenth (10) Day of the Solo -Quarantine Experience Celebrate - Thankfulness

Gratitude, thankfulness or gratefulness a feeling of appreciation felt by and/or similar positive response shown by a recipient.

Goal I: Gain Peace and Gratitude

Part 1 Spiritual Health Happy and Love Connected Challenge
10 minutes

Part 2 Meditation Experiences
'Giving Praise Experience'

Biblical Scripture

> It is a good thing to give thanks unto the Lord, and to sing praises unto thy name O most High.
>
> PSALM 92:1

Meditate on 10 Good Thoughts that make you feel happy and lovely.

Goal II: Stimulate the Brain Cells

Part 1 Mental Health Challenge
40 minutes

Part 2 Recitation Experience
Name 25 types of cars

Goal III: Get the Body into Motion

Part 1 -Physical Health Challenge
40 minutes

Part 2 – Exercise Activity
'Ham Hock Kicks'-
Using a straight back chair(seated) - kicks in a chair; kick each leg 50 times within time limit.

SHOUT HALLELUJAH!

(See Hints -Type of Cars

1. Ford
2. Chevrolet
3. Cadillac
4. Mercedes
5. Dodge
6. Subaru
7. Mitsubishi
8. BMW
9. Volvo
10. Toyota
11. GMC
12. Mini -Cooper
13. Porsche
14. Kia

15. Bentley
16. Mercedes
17. Jaguar
18. MGB
19. Van
20. Lexus
21. Sedan
22. 4-door
23. Lamborghini
24. Chrysler
25. Volkswagon
26. Hunydanui

CHAPTER 11

FEEL -GOOD WORD OF THE DAY: CHARITY

On the Eleventh(11) Day of the Solo-Quarantine Experience Celebrate - Charity

Def Generosity and helpfulness especially toward the needy or suffering

Goal I: Gain Peace and Gratitude

Part 1 Spiritual Health Happy and Love Connected Challenge: 10 minutes

Part 2 Meditation Experience
'The Charity Experience'
Meditate on the love chapter(Holy Bible).

Biblical Scriptures

1-Though I speak with the tongues of men and of angels and have not charity. I am become a sounding brass or a tinkling cymbals.

2 And though I have the gift if prophecy, and understand all mysteries, and all knowledge; and though I have all faith, so that I could removed mountains, and have not charity, I am nothing.

3 And though I bestow all my goods to feed the poor and though I give my body to be burned, and have not charity, it profiteth me nothing

4. Charity suffereth long, and is kind: charity envieth not: charity vaunteth not itself, is not puffed up.

5 Doth not behave itself unseemly, seeketh not her own, is not easily provoked, thinketh no evil;

6 Rejoiceth, not in iniquity, but rejoiceth in the truth.

7 Beareth all things, believeth all things, hopeth all things endureth all things.

8 Charity, never faileth: but whether there be prophecies, they shall fall: whether there be tongues, they shall cease; whether there be knowledge, it shall vanish away,

9 For we know in part, and we prophesy in part,

10 But when that which is perfect is come, then that which is in part shall be done away.

11 When I was a child, I spake as a child, I understood as a child, but when I became a man, I put away childish things

12 For now, we see through a glass, darkly: but then face to face: now I know in part: but then shall I know even as also I am known.

13 And now abideth faith, hope and charity, these three;
but the greatest of these is charity.

I CORORINTHIANS 13:1-13

Meditate on 10 acts of charity that give you feelings Of happiness and loving.

Goal II: Stimulate Brain Cells

Part 1 Mental Health Challenge
40 minutes

Part 2 Recitation Experience
Name 20 flowers that bloom
(Hints on flowers)

Goal 3: Get the Body in Motion

Part 1. Physical Health Challenge
40 minutes

Part 2. Exercise Activity
'Perch Fish Play in the River' -Simulate Jumping rope 50 times

SHOUT HALLELUJAH!

(Hints- Flowers that Bloom)

1. Roses
2. Lilies
3. Orchids
4. Daisy
5. Marigolds
6. Honeysuckles
7. Carnations
8. Violets

9. Crysthanamums
10. Peonies
11. Tulips
12. Dahlias
13. Gladiolus
14. Begonia
15. Lavender
16. Zinnias
17. Sunflower
18. Hydrangea
19. Impatients
20. Baby Breaths

CHAPTER 12

FEEL- GOOD WORD OF THE DAY: RESPONSIBLE

On the Twelfth (12) Day of the Solo-Quarantine Experience Celebrate Responsible

Having an obligation to do something or having control over or care for someone, as part of one's job or role.

Goal I: Gain Peace and Gratitude

Part 1 Spiritual Health Happy and Love Connected Challenge
10 minutes

Part 2 Meditation Experience
'Red Sea Experience'-Moses Responsible for The Jewish Crossings

Biblical Scripture

> Lift thou up, thy rod, and stretch out thine hand over the sea, and divide it: and the children of Israel shall go on dry ground through the midst of the sea.
>
> EXODUS 14:16

Meditate on 10 rewards of happiness and love you
Received after meditating on the experience.

Goal II: Stimulate Brain Cells

Part 1. Mental Health Challenge
40 minutes

Part 2. Recitation Experiences
Name 10 breeds of horses from around the world
(See Hints)

Goal III: Set the Body in Motion

Part 1. Physical Health Challenge
40 minutes challenge

Part 2. Exercise Activity
'Eel Maneuvers'
Stand-up straight and simulate 50 Backstroke swimming maneuvers.

SHOUT HALLELUJAH!

(Hints Breeds of Horses)
10 Breeds of Horses

1. Paint
2. Quarter
3. Race
4. Arabians
5. Palomino
6. Clydesdale
7. Mustang
8. Thoroughbred
9. Bay
10. Appaloosas

CHAPTER 13

FEEL- GOOD WORD OF THE DAY: FAITH

On the Thirteenth (13) Day of the Solo-Quarantine Experience Celebrate Faith

Def is confidence or trust in a person, thing or concept, in the context of religion, one can define faith as "belief in God"

Goal I: Gain Peace and Gratitude

Part 1. Spiritual Health Happy and Love Connected Challenge
10 minutes

Part 2. Meditation Experience
'Faith Experience'

Faith -Embrace 10 positive personal experiences with faith. Find happy and love feelings within the meditation.

Biblical Scripture

> Now faith is the substance of things hope far, the evidence of things not seen.
>
> HEBREW 11:1

Goal II: Stimulate Brain Cells

Part 1. Mental Health Challenge
40 minutes

Part 2. Recitation Experiences
Recite 25 popular girl's name

Goal III: Get the Body in Motion

Part 1. Physical Health Challenge
40 minutes

Part 2. Exercise Activity
'Solo Dancing' -Using a doorknob as a partner- Simulate fast dancing for 50 minutes.

SHOUT HALLELUJAH!

(Hint -Popular Girls' names)

1. Janice
2. Kim
3. Mary
4. Jennifer
5. Michelle
6. Amber
7. Gayle
8. Felecia
9. Annette
10. Joy
11. Linda
12. Louisa
13. Patricia
14. Lucy
15. Dana

16. Judy
17. Betty
18. Teresa
19. Carol
20. Alice
21. Lydia
22. Lacey
23. Karen
24. Denice
25. Ellen

CHAPTER 14

FEEL -GOOD WORD OF THE DAY: COMMAND

On the Fourteenth(14) Day of Solo-Quarantine Experiences - Celebrate -Command

Def as an order given.

Goal I: Gain Patience and Gratitude

Part 1. Spiritual Health Challenge Happy and Love Connected Challenge

10 minutes

Part 2 Meditation Experience

'Centurion Command Experience'

Biblical Scripture

> And Jesus said unto the centurion, Go thy way: and as thou hast believed, so be it done unto thee. And his servant was healed in the self-same hour.
>
> MATTHEW 8:13

Meditate on 10 feelings of satisfaction with authorities
That brought you happiness and love during your career
After dealing with a boss.

Goal II: Stimulate the Brain Cells

Part 1. Mental Health Challenge
40 minutes

Part 2. Recitation Experience
Name 25 veterans from all branches of service
(See Hints -Branches of Service)

Goal III: Get the Body in Motion

Part 1. Physical Health Challenge
40 minutes

Part 2. Exercise Activity
'Member of the Band' Simulate -100 Marching Steps -in- Place

SHOUT HALLELUJAH!

(See Veteran Hints)

1. Army
2. Navy
3. Air Force
4. Marine
5. Coast Guard

CHAPTER 15

FEEL -GOOD WORD OF THE DAY: BLESSINGS

On the Fifteenth(15) Day of Solo-Quarantine Experience-Celebrate-Blessings

Def God's protection and favor and positive gifts

Goal I: Gain Peace and Gratitude

Part 1. Spiritual Health Happy and Love Connected Challenge
10 minutes

Part 2. Meditation Experience
Meditate on spiritual revelations
'Isle of Patmos Experience'

Biblical Scripture

> I, John who also am your brother, and companion in tribulation, and in the Kingdom and patience of Jesus Christ, was in the Isle that is called Patmos, for the word of God, and for the testimony of Jesus Christ
>
> THE REVELATION 1:9

Meditate on 10 happy and love blessings you receive from the study of the Isle of Patmos.

Goal II: Stimulate the Brain Cells

Part 1. Mental Health Challenge
40 minutes

Part 2. Recitation Experiences
Recite the names of 25 types of vegetables.
(See Hints for vegetables)

Goal III: Get the Body in Motion

Part 1. Physical Health Challenge
40 minutes

Part 2. Exercise Activity

'Easter- Bunny- Hopping' Time- While holding onto the back of the straight back chair- Hop on your left leg 25 times and switch and hop on your right leg 25 times.

SHOUT HALLELUJAH!

Hints 50 types of vegetables

1. Asparagus
2. Beets
3. Celery
4. Cabbage
5. Kale
6. Collards
7. Carrots
8. Mustard Greens
9. Red Onions
10. Green Beans

11. Cucumbers
12. Radishes
13. Squash
14. Leeks
15. Green Peas
16. Blackeyed Peas
17. Tomatoes
18. Pinto Beans
19. Okra
20. Corn
21. Lima Beans
22. Green Pepper
23. Hot Pepper
24. White onions
25. Garlic

CHAPTER 16

FEEL -GOOD WORD OF THE DAY: WELLNESS

On the Sixteenth(16) Day of Solo-Quarantine Celebrate Wellness

Def Wellness definition the quality or state of being healthy in body and mind, especially as the result of deliberate effort.

Goal I. Gain Peace and Gratitude

Part 1. Spiritual Health Happy and Love Challenge
10 minutes

Part 2 Meditation Experience:
'Malita Experience'

Biblical Scriptures

1-And when they were escaped then they knew that the Island was called Melita

2-And the barbarous people shewed us no little kindness: Fir they kindled a fire, and received us every one, because of the present rain, and because of the cold.

> 3 And when Paul had gathered a bundle of sticks, and laid them on the fire, there came a viper out of the heat, and fastened on his hand.
>
> 4. And when the barbarians saw the venomous beast hang among themselves no doubt this man is a murderer, whom, though he hath escaped thc sea, yea vengeance suffereth not to live.
>
> 5 And he shook off the beast unto the fire, and felt no harm.
>
> 7. Howbeit they looked when he should have swollen, or fallen down dead suddenly: but after they had looked a great while, and saw no harm come to him, they changed their minds, and said that he was a god.
>
> ACTS 28:2-5, 7

Meditate on 10 positive happy and lovely health experiences that you recall after Reading the scriptures.

Goal II. Stimulate Brain Cells

Part 1. Mental Health Challenge
40 minutes

Part 2. Recitation Experience
Name Common Islands in North America
(See Hints)

Goal III. Get the Body in Motion

Part 1. Physical Health Challenge
40 minutes

Part 2. Exercise Activity
Praise Claps -Clap your hands 100 times

SHOUT HALLELUJAH!

Hints – North America Islands

1. Jamaica
2. Bahamas
3. Anguilla
4. Antigua and Barbuda
5. Aruba
6. Barbados
7. Belize
8. Bermuda
9. Bonaire
10. British Virgin Island
11. Canada
12. Cayman Islands
13. Clippertin Island
14. Costa Rica
15. Cuba
16. Curacao
17. Dominica
18. Dominican Republic
19. El Salvador
20. Venezuela
21. Grenda
22. Guadeloupe
23. Guatemala
24. Haiti
25. Honduras
26. Martinique
27. Mexico
28. Montserrat
29. Nicaragua

30. Venezuela
31. Panama
32. Puerto Rico
33. Saba
34. Colombia
35. Saint Barthelemy
36. Saint Kitts and Nevis
37. Saint Lucia
38. Saint Martin
39. Saint Pierre and Miquellon
40. Saint Vincent and the Grenadines
41. Sint Eustitus
42. Trinidad and Tobago
43. Turks and Cacos Island
44. United States
45. United States Virgin Island

CHAPTER 17

FEEL -GOOD WORD OF THE DAY: HELP

On the Seventeenth(17) Day on Solo -Quarantine Experiences Celebrate - Help

Def Do something by offering one's services or resources

Goal I. Gain Peace and Gratitude

Part 1. Spiritual Health and Love Connected Challenge
10 minutes

Part 2. Meditation Experience
Help
"Good Blessings Experience'

Biblical Scripture

> I have been young, and now am old; I have not seen the righteous forsaken, nor his seed begging bread.
>
> PSALM 37:25

Meditate on 10 remembrances of good feelings of happiness and love you got after helping individuals.

Goal II: Stimulate Brain Cells

Part 1. Mental Health Challenge
40 minutes

Part 2. Recitation Experiences
Recite the names of 25 appliances

Goal III: Get the Body in Motion

Part 1. Physical Health Challenge
40 minutes

Part 2. Exercise Activity
'Neck Wrangler'- Twist the Neck from left to right 50 times and then 50 times from Right to left .
SHOUT HALLELUJAH!

Hints -25 Appliances

1. Refrigerator
2. Stoves
3. Blender
4. Food Processor
5. Knife Sharper
6. Freezers
7. Ice Cream Freezers
8. Knife Sharpers
9. Juicers
10. Toaster
11. Warm ovens
12. Jar Opener

13. Can Opener
14. Electric Skillet
15. Electric Knife
16. Microwave oven
17. Egg Poacher
18. Deep Fat Fryer
19. Chicken Roaster
20. Turkey Cooker
21. Electric Slow Cooker
22. Fish Cooker
23. Canner
24. Water Bath for steaming vegetables
25. Food Warmer
26. Corn popper
27. Dishwasher
28. Steak Grill
29. Garbage Disposal
30. Dishwasher

CHAPTER 18

FEEL- GOOD WORD OF THE DAY: PURPOSE

On the Eighteenth (18) Day of the Solo-Quarantine Challenge – Celebrate -Purpose

Def The reason for which something is done or created or for which something exists

Goal I: Gain Peace and Gratitude

Part 1 – Spiritual Health and Happy and Love Connected Challenge 10 minutes

Part 2 – Meditation Experience
'Signs of Individual's Purpose and Seasons'

Biblical Scriptures

> 1-To every thing there is a season, and a time to every purpose under the heaven;
>
> 2-A time to be born, and a time to die; a time to plant and a time to pluck up that which is planted;

3-A time to kill, and a time to heal; a time to break down, and a time to build up:

4 -A time to weep, and a time to laugh: a time to mourn, and a time to dance.

5- A time to cast away stones, and a time to gather stones together: a time to embrace, and a time to refrain from embracing.

6 -A time to get and a time to lose; a time to keep, and a time to cast away.

7- A time to read, and a time to sew; a time to keep silence, and a time to speak;

8- A time to love, and a time to hate; a time of war, and a time of peace

Meditate on 10 feelings of purpose of happiness and loving within the seasons according to

Your purpose.
ECCLESIASTICS 3:1-8

Goal II. Stimulate Brain Cells

Part 1 – Mental Health Challenge
40 minutes

Part 2 -Recitation Challenge
Recite 50 types of languages
(See Languages)

Goal III. Get the Body in Motion

Part 1. Physical Health Challenge
40 minutes

Part 2. Exercise Activity
Marathon Runner -Simulate Running A 40 -minutes marathon -in-place

SHOUT HALLELUJAH!

(Hints - Languages)

1. Afrikaans
2. Arabic
3. Bangla
4. Bosnian (Latin)
5. Bulgarian
6. Catalan
7. Chinese (simplified)
8. Chinese(Traditional)
9. Croatian
10. Czech
11. Danish
12. 12.Dutch
13. English
14. Estonian
15. Filipino
16. Finnish
17. French
18. German
19. Greek
20. Gujarati
21. Haitian Creole
22. Hebrew
23. Hindi
24. Hungarian
25. Icelandic

26. Indonesian
27. Irish
28. Japanese
29. Kannada
30. Kazakh
31. Kiswahili
32. Korean
33. Kurdish
34. Latvian
35. Lithuanian
36. Malagasy
37. Malay
38. Malayalam
39. Maltelsa
40. Maon
41. Marathi
42. Norwegian
43. Odia
44. Pashto
45. Persian(Afghanistan)
46. Persian
47. Polish
48. Portuguese(Portugal)
49. Punjabi
50. Romanian
51. Russian
52. Samoan
53. Serbian(Cyrillic)
54. Serbian (Latin)
55. Slovak
56. Slovenian
57. Spanish
58. Swahili
59. Swedish
60. Tamil
61. Telugu

62. Thai
63. Tongan
64. Turkish
65. Ukrainian
66. Urdu
67. Vietnamese
68. Welsh

CHAPTER 19

FEEL -GOOD WORD OF THE DAY: EDUCATION

On the Eighteenth (18) Day of the Solo-Quarantine Experience-Celebrate -Education

Def education is the process of facilitating learning or the acquisition of knowledge, skills, values, morals, beliefs and habits. Educational methods include teaching, training, telling stories, research and many other methods.

Goal I. Gain Peace and Gratitude

Part1. Spiritual Health Happy and Love Challenge
10 minutes

Part 2. Meditation Experience
'Timothy's Educational Experience'

Biblical Scriptures

1 Then came he to Derbe and Lystra and, behold, a certain disciple was there, named Timotheus, the son of a certain woman, which was a Jewess, and believed, but his father was a Greek.

3 Him would Paul have to go forth with him, and took and circumcised him because of the Jews which were in those quarters: for they knew all that his father was a Greek.

4. And as they went through the cities, they delivered them the decrees for to keep, that were ordained of the apostles and elders Jerusalem which were of Jrey.

ACTS 16:1-4

Meditate on 10 ways you have been a good student as a result of good teachers who made you feel happy and love.

Goal II. Stimulate the Brain Cells

Part 1. Mental Health Challenge
40 minutes

Part 2. Recitation Challenge
Recite capitals cities of U.S. States
(See Hints -State Capitals Cities)

Goal III. Get the Body in Motion

Part 1. Physical Health Challenge
40 minutes

Part 2. Exercise Activity
'Bath Towel See -Saw Motions' -Using a bath towel-Do 50 windmill actions from left to right using an over the head action.

SHOUT HALLELUJAH!

(Hints – 50 U.S. States Capital Cities)

1. Montgomery-AL
2. Juneau -AK
3. Phoenix-AZ
4. Little Rock-AR
5. Sacramento-CA
6. Denver-CO
7. Hartford -CT
8. Dover-DE
9. Tallahassee-FL
10. Honolulu-HI
11. Atlanta-GA
12. Boise-ID
13. Springfield-IL
14. Indianapolis-IN
15. Des Moines-IA
16. Topeka-KS
17. Frankfort-KY
18. Baton Rouge-LA
19. Augusta-ME
20. Annapolis-MD
21. Boston-MA
22. Lansing- MI
23. Saint Paul-MN
24. Jackson-MS
25. Jefferson City-MO
26. Helena-MT
27. Lincoln-NE
28. Concord-NH
29. Trenton-NJ
30. Santa Fe-NM
31. Albany- NY
32. Raleigh-NC
33. Bismarck-ND
34. Columbus-OH

35. Oklahoma City-OK
36. Salem -OR
37. Harrisburg-PA
38. Providence -RI
39. Columbia-SC
40. Pierre-SD
41. Nashville -TN
42. Austin-TX
43. Salt Lake City-UT
44. Richmond -VA
45. Olympia-WA
46. Charleston-WV
47. Montpelier-VT
48. Olympia -WA
49. Madison-Wisconsin
50. Laramie -WY

CHAPTER 20

FEEL- GOOD WORD OF THE DAY: TRAVEL

On the Twentieth (20) Day of the Solo-Quarantine Experience -Celebrate Travel

Goal I: Gain Peace and Gratitude

Part 1. Spiritual Health Happy and Love
Challenge
10 minutes

Part 2. Meditation Experience
Travel
'The Magi Experience'

Biblical Scriptures

> 12 And being warned of God and in a dream that they should not return to Herod, my departed into their own country another way

> 13 And when they were departed behold, the angel of the LORD appeareth to Joseph in a dream, saying, Arise, and take the young child and his mother and flee into Egypt, and be those there until I bring thee word for Herod will seek the young child destroy him.
>
> MATHEW 2:1-12

Meditate on 10 good feelings of happiness and love after you have read the scripture about
Finding a savior.

Goal II. Stimulate Brain Cells

Part 1. Mental Health Challenge
40 minutes

Part 2. Recitation Experience
Name States with ports
(see hints)

Goal III. Get the Body in Motion

Part 1. Physical Health Challenge
40 minutes

Part 2. Exercise Activity
Juggling Simulation -Simulate juggling two balls for 50 minutes

SHOUT HALLELUJAH!

(States with Ports)

1. Alabama
2. Alaska
3. California
4. Georgia

5. Florida
6. Hawaii
7. Louisiana
8. Maine
9. Minnesota
10. Missouri
11. Mississippi
12. North Carolina
13. Oklahoma
14. Pennsylvania
15. South Carolina
16. Texas
17. Virginia
18. West Virginia
19. South Carolina
20. Washington

CHAPTER 21

FEEL- GOOD WORD OF THE DAY: NATURE

On the Twenty-First (21) Day of the Solo- Quarantine Experience- Celebrate – Nature

Def the natural, physical, material world or universe

Goal I. Gain Peace and Gratitude

Part 1. Spiritual Health Happy and Love Connected Challenge
10 minutes

Part 2. Meditation Experience
'Jehovah -jireh Experience' -Nature

Biblical Scripture

> And Abraham called the name of that place Jehovah-jireh: as it is said to this day. In the mount of the Lord it shall being seen.
>
> GENESIS 22:14

Meditate on 10 miracles in your life that gave you happiness and love.

Goal II. Stimulate the Brain Cells

Part 1. Mental Health Challenge
40 minutes

Part 2. Recitation Experience
Name 25 species of trees
(see Hints-names of trees)

Goal III. Get the Body in Motion

Part 1. Physical Health Challenge
40 minutes

Part 2. Exercise Activity

'Mountain Climbing' – Using your chair, step up in the seat of the chair 50 times each with the right and left legs.

SHOUT HALLELUJAH!

(See Hints-Names of trees)

1. Elm
2. Cedar
3. Oak
4. Pine
5. Willow
6. Cottonwood
7. Maple
8. Redwood
9. Pecan
10. Cherry
11. Walnut
12. Peach
13. Apple
14. Fig

15. Blackjack
16. Apricot
17. Fir
18. Pear
19. Mulberry
20. Hickory
21. Sierra
22. Pine
23. Mimosa
24. Apple
25. Birch

CHAPTER 22

FEEL -GOOD WORD OF THE DAY: THANKSGIVING

On the Twenty-Second(22) Day of the Solo-Quarantine Experience Celebrate -Thanksgiving

Thanksgiving is a national holiday, celebrated as a day of giving thanks and sacrifice for God's blessings.

Goal I. Gain Peace and Gratitude

Part 1. Spiritual Health Happy and Love - Connected Challenge
10 minutes

Part 2. Meditation Experience
'Give thanks for Everything Experience'

Biblical Scripture

> Be careful for nothing but in everything in prayer and supplication with thanksgiving.
>
> PHILLIPIANS 4:5

Meditate of 10 good feelings of happy and love after giving thanks for good deeds.

Goal II. Stimulate Brain Cells

Part 1. Mental Health Challenge
40 minutes

Part 2. Recitation Experience
Recite 25 good gifts you have physical, mental or emotional

Goal III. Get the Body in Motion

Part I. Physical Health Challenge
40 minutes

Part II. Exercise Activity
Basketball Hoops Simulation – Simulate shooting a basketball 100 times using motion of Raising the basketball from the floor and shooting toward the goal.

SHOUT HALLELUJAH!

CHAPTER 23

FEEL -GOOD WORD OF THE DAY: RELAXATION

On the Twenty-Third(23) Day of the Solo-Quarantine Experience – Celebrate Relaxation

Def Relaxation is a process that decreases the effects of stress on your mind and body. Peace from anger or anxiety

Goal I. Gain Peace and Gratitude

Part 1. Spiritual Health Happy and
Love Connected Challenge
10 minutes

Part 2. Meditation Experience
'The Daniel Experience'

Biblical Scripture

> Then was the king exceeding glad for him, and commanded that they should take Daniel up out of the den. So Daniel was taken up out of the den, and no manner of hurt was found upon him, because he believed in God.
>
> DANIEL 6:23

Meditate on 10 good feelings of happy and love after being released from a terrible situation.

Goal II. Stimulate Brain Cells

Part 1. Mental Health Challenge
40 minutes

Part 2. Recitation Experience
Recite the names of 25 types of religions
(see Hints-Types of Religions)

Goal III. Get the Body in Motion

Part 1. Physical Health Challenge
40 minutes

Part 2. Exercise Activity
'Winemaker's Stomps' – Simulate mashing grapes in a barrel for 100 times on each leg.

SHOUT HALLELUJAH!

Hints – Types of Religions

1. Christianity
2. Judaism
3. Buddhism

4. Hinduism
5. Taoism
6. Islam
7. Sikhism
8. Mormonism
9. Atheism
10. Juche
11. Spiritism
12. Baha'i
13. Shinto
14. Caodaism
15. Rastafarian
16. Amish
17. Agnostics
18. Animism
19. Zen
20. Confucianism
21. Hare Krishna
22. Humanism
23. Jehovah's Witness
24. Mennonite
25. Paganism
26. Voodoo
27. Witchcraft
28. Salvation Army
29. Scientology
30. Spiritualism
31. Sun worship

CHAPTER 24

FEEL GOOD WORD(S) OF THE DAY: FRUIT OF THE SPIRIT

On the Twentieth-Fourth (24) Day of Solo-Quarantine Experience-Celebrate -Fruit of the Spirit

Def the Fruit of the Holy Spirit is a biblical term that sums up nine attributes of a person or community living in accord with the Holy Spirit, according to chapter 5 of the Epistle of the Galatians: "But the fruit of Spirit of love, joy, peace, patience, kindness, goodness, faithfulness, gentleness

Goal I. Gain Peace and Gratitude

Part 1. Spiritual Health Happy and Love Connected Challenge
10 minutes

Part 2. Meditation Experience
'Gifts of the Spirit Experience'

Biblical Scriptures

> 22 But the fruit of the Spirit is love, joy, peace, longsuffering, gentleness, goodness, faith
>
> 23 meekness, temperance, against such there is no law.
>
> GALATIANS 5:22,23

Meditate on 10 methods to daily achieve the fruit of the Spirit and get happy and love.

Goal II. Stimulate the Brain Cells

Part 1. Mental Health Challenge
40 minutes

Part 2. Recitation Experience
Recite 25 different types of fruits
(See Hints)

Goal III. Get the Body in Motion

Part 1. Physical Health Challenge
40 minutes

Part 2. Exercise Activity
'Running Worm Crawl' -Simulate crawling like a worm in a hurry for 50 minutes.

SHOUT HALLELUJAH!

(See Fruit Hints)

Hints Different Types of Fruits

1. Apples
2. Bananas
3. Bing cherries
4. Blueberries
5. Blackberries
6. Cantaloupes
7. Cherries
8. Cranberries
9. Currants
10. Dewberries
11. Figs
12. Grapefruits
13. Grapes
14. Honeydew
15. Kiwi
16. Kumquats
17. Mango
18. Lemons
19. limes
20. Mandarins
21. Mulberries
22. nectarines
23. Oranges
24. Papayas
25. Peaches
26. Pears
27. Persimmons
28. Plums
29. Raspberries
30. Strawberries
31. Tangerines
32. tangelos
33. Watermelons

CHAPTER 25

FEEL- GOOD WORD OF THE DAY: COURAGE

On the Twenty-Fifth (25) Day of the Solo Quarantine Experience Celebrate- Courage

Def the ability to do something that frightens one or ability to do something that is difficult or dangerous

Goal I: Gain Peace and Gratitude

Part 1. Spiritual Health Happy and Love Challenge
10 Minutes

Part 2. Meditation Experience
'Young David Experience'
David Killed Goliath

Biblical Scriptures

50 So David prevailed over the philistine with a sling and with a stone, and smote the philistine, and slew him: but there was no sword in the hand of David.

51 Therefore David ran, and stood upon the philistine, and took his sword, and drew it out of the sheath and drew it out of the sheath And slew him, and cut off his head therewith. Had when the Philistines saw their champion was dead, they fled.

56 And the king said, Inquire thou whose son the stripling is.

57 And as David returned from slaughter of the Philistine Abner took him, and brought him before Saul with the head of the Philistine in his hand.

58 And Saul said to him, whose son art thou, thou young man? And David answered. I am the son of thy servant Jessie, the Bethlehemite.

I SAMUEL 17:50, 51; 56-58

Meditate on 10 good experiences you have during your childhood that made you happy and loving.

Goal II. Stimulate the Brain Cells

Part 1. Mental Health Challenge
40 minutes

Part 2. Recitation Experience
Recite the Names of Common Zoo animals
(See Hints)

Goal III. Get the Body in Motion

Part 1. Physical Health Challenge
40 minutes

Part 2. Exercise Activity

Baseball Batter's Swing – Simulate swing the bat 50 times on the left and 50 times on the right.

SHOUT HALLELUJAH!

(Hints-Animals in a Zoo)

1. Monkeys
2. Zebras
3. Camels
4. Tigers
5. Peacocks
6. Wolves
7. Elephants
8. Orangutans
9. Gorillas
10. Foxes
11. Lizards
12. Hippopotamus
13. Giraffes
14. Boa Constrictors
15. Apes
16. Lions
17. Macaws
18. Pandas
19. Polar Bears
20. Snakes
21. Turtles
22. Grizzly Bears
23. Rhinoceros
24. Alligator
25. Crocodile

CHAPTER 26

FEEL- GOOD WORD OF THE DAY: STRENGTH

On the Twentieth-Sixth (26) Day of the Solo-Quarantine Experience Celebrate -Strength

Def the quality or state of being physically strong

Goal I: Gain Peace and Gratitude

Part 1: Spiritual Health
Happy and Love Connected Challenge
10 minutes

Part 2. Meditation Experience
'Regaining of Strength Experience'
Sampson and Delilah
Where did he get his strength?

Biblical Scriptures

> 10 And Delilah said unto Samson, Behold, thou hast mocked me, and told me lies: now, tell me, I pray thee, wherewith thou mightiest be bound.

> 17 That he told her all his heart, and said unto her, There hath not come a razor upon my head: for I have been Nazarite unto God from my mother's womb: if I be shaven then my strength will go from me, and I shall become weak, and I shall become weak, and be like any other man.
>
> JUDGES 16:10,17

Meditate on 10 feelings of strength you remember you have that brought you happy and love.

Goal II: Stimulate Brain Cells

Part 1. Mental Health Challenge
40 minutes

Part 2. Recitation Experience
Recite the names of 25 types of entrees or meat dishes.
(See Hints-Types of Entrees)

Goal III. Get the Body in Motion

Part 1. Physical Health Challenge
40 minutes

Part 2. Exercise Activity
Toddlers' Pushups -Get on your mat- an simulate one hand push-ups-50 on each side.

SHOUT HALLELUJAH!

Hints -Types of Entrees or Meat Dishes

1. Meat Loaf
2. Chicken Fried Steak
3. Chicken Loaf
4. Tuna Casserole

5. Barbecue Ribs
6. Fried Chicken
7. Smoked Brisket
8. Smoked Chicken
9. Broiled Chicken
10. Baked Barbecue Chicken
11. Baked Trout
12. Fried Fish
13. Fried Oysters
14. Roasted Turkey
15. Roasted Beef
16. Smothered Liver
17. Swedish Meatballs
18. Spaghetti and Meat Sauce
19. Lemon Baked Fish
20. Sauerkraut and Bratwursts
21. Chicken Pot Pie
22. Shepherd's Pie
23. Beef and Onions
24. Pot Roast
25. Beef Stroganoff

CHAPTER 27

FEEL GOOD WORD OF THE DAY: FELLOWSHIP

On the Twentieth-Seventh(27) Day of the Solo-Quarantine Experience - Celebrate

Fellowship

Def. companionship, company

Goal I. Gain Peace and Gratitude

Part 1. Spiritual Health Happy and Love Connected Challenge 10 minutes

Part2. Meditation Experience

'Invisible Strength Experience'

Biblical Scriptures

I can do all things through Christ who strengthenth me
PHILIPPIANS 4:13

Beware of Dogs, beware of evil workers, beware of the concision.

PHILLIPIANS 3:2

Goal II. Stimulate Brain Cells

Part 1. Mental Health Challenge
40 minutes

Part 2. Recitation Expense
Name 25 boys' names
(You write these down)

Goal III. Get the Body in Motion

Part 1. Physical Health Challenge
40 minutes

Part 2. Exercise Activity
'Shoulder to Toe Maneuvers' – Stand straight, touch your shoulders and then your toes for 100 times

SHOUT HALLELUJAH!

(Hints -Boys' names)

1. Dan
2. Ben
3. David
4. James
5. Jack
6. Henry
7. Jerry
8. George
9. Barry

10. Sam
11. Joe
12. Ken
13. Andy
14. Keith
15. Jared
16. Jeremy
17. Timothy
18. John
19. George
20. Jimmy
21. Earl
22. Stephen
23. Ken
24. Ted
25. Lloyd

CHAPTER 28

FEEL -GOOD WORD OF THE DAY: GENEROUS

On the Twentieth-eighth (28) Day of the Solo-Quarantine Experience - Celebrate Generous

Showing a readiness to give more of something, as money or time, that is strictly necessary or expected

Goal I: Gain Peace and Gratitude

Part 1. Spiritual Health Happy and
Love Connected Challenge
10 minutes

Part 2. Meditation Experience
' Jeremiah Experience -known before birth'

Biblical Scripture

> Before I formed thee in the belly, I knew thee.
>
> JEREMIAH 1:5

Meditate on 10 goals you have achieved and made you happy and loving.

Goal II. Stimulate the Brain Cells

Part 1. Mental Health Challenge
40 minutes

Part 2. Recitation Experience
Name 25 Species of Birds
(see Hints -Types of Birds)

Goal III. Get the Body in Motion

Part 1. Physical Health Challenge
40 minutes

Part 2. Exercise Activity
'Birds Flying' -Flap Arms and run in circles for 40 minutes

SHOUT HALLELUJAH!

(Hints -Types of Birds)

1. Owl
2. Peacock
3. Red Bird
4. Blue Jay
5. Quail
6. Peacock
7. Yellow bird
8. Wood pecker
9. Parrot
10. Blue bird
11. Cardinal
12. Black bird

13. Hawks
14. Eagles
15. Crows
16. Seagull
17. Pelicans
18. Flamingo
19. Egrets
20. Parrakeet
21. Macaw
22. Pigeon
23. Buzzard
24. Duck
25. Hummingbird

CHAPTER 29

FEEL -GOOD WORD OF THE DAY: PEACE

On the Twentieth -Ninth(29) Day of the Solo-Quarantine Experience- Celebrate Peace

Def a state of tranquility or quiet lack of violence, conflict

Goal I: Gain Peace and Gratitude

Part 1. Spiritual Health Happy and Love
Connected Challenge
10 minutes

Part 2. Meditation Experience
'Peace by the Protector Experience'

Biblical Scriptures

1 The Lord is my Shepherd, I shall not want

2 He maketh me to lie down in green pastures: He leadeth me beside the still waters.

3 He restoreth my soul: he leadeth me in the paths of righteousness for his name's sake.

1 Yea, though I walk through the valley of the shadow of death, I will far no evil; for thou art with me; thy rod and thy staff they comfort me.

2 Thou preparest a table before me in the presence of mine enemies those anointest my head with oil; my cup Runneth over.

6. Surely goodness and mercy shall follow me all the days of my life, and I will dwell in the house of the Lord for ever.

PSALM 23:1-6

Meditate on 10 Peaceful situations you have had in your near environment that resulted in happiness and love.

Goal II. Stimulate the Brain Cells

Part 1. Mental Health Challenge
40 minutes

Part 2. Recitation Experience
Name 20 breeds of Dogs
(Hints-See Breeds of Dogs)

Goal III. Get the Body in Motion

Part 1. Physical Health Challenge
40 minutes

Part 2. Exercise Activity
Slow Strolling Solo Strollers- Simulate a slow stroll trot through the woods for 50 minutes

SHOUT HALLELUJAH!

Hint - Breeds of Dogs

1. Cocker Spaniel
2. Terrier
3. Doberman
4. Poodle
5. Pit bull
6. Pomeranian
7. Pug
8. Chow Chow
9. Bird Dog
10. Collie
11. Basset Hound
12. St. Bernard
13. Miniature Schnauzer
14. Rottweiler
15. Afghan Hound
16. German Shepherd
17. Beagles
18. Labrador
19. Golden Retriever
20. Shih Tzu
21. English Mashiff
22. Beagles
23. Yorkie
24. Australian Cattle Dog
25. Maltese

CHAPTER 30

FEEL GOOD WORD OF THE DAY: LAUGHTER

On the thirtieth (30) Day of the Solo-Quarantine Experience- Celebrate - Laughter

Def the act of action or sound after a happy exercise

Goal I: Gain Peace and Gratitude

Part 1. Spiritual Health Happy and Love
Connected Challenge
10 minutes

Part 2. Meditation Experience
'Sarah Experience'

Biblical Scripture

> And Sarah said, God hath made me to laugh, so that all that hear will laugh with me.
>
> GENESIS 21:6

Meditate on 10 happenings that give you feelings of being happy and in love.

Goal II: Stimulate the Brain Cells

Part 1. Mental Health Challenge
40 minutes

Part 2. Recitation Experience
Recite the names of twenty -five cakes
(see Hints)

Goal III: Get the Body in Motion

Part 1. Physical Health Challenge
40 minutes

Part 2. Exercise Activity

Whirlwind Exercise – Holding the back of the chair, simulate making 50 circular whirls on the right leg,

Change to the left leg and make 50 circular whirls.

SHOUT HALLELUJAH!

(Hints - Types of Cakes)

1. Coconut Cake
2. Lemon Cake
3. Lime Cake
4. Pineapple Cake
5. Apple Cake
6. Spice Cake
7. German Chocolate Cake
8. Lava Cake
9. Jelly Cake
10. Banana Cake

11. Caramel Cake
12. Japanese Cake
13. Fruit Cake
14. Pound Cake
15. Nut Cake
16. Peanut Butter Cake
17. Angel Food Cake
18. Baked Alaska
19. Cherry Cake
20. Strawberry Cake
21. Carrot Cake
22. Chocolate Chip Cake
23. Pineapple Upside Down Cake
24. Fig Cake
25. Yellow Cake
26. Marble Cake

CHAPTER 31

FEEL- GOOD WORD OF THE DAY: BELIEF

On the Thirtieth -first (31) Day of the Solo-Quarantine Experience Celebrate -Belief

Def an acceptance that statement is true or that something exists

Goal I: Gain Peace and Gratitude

Part 1. Spiritual Health Happy and Love Challenge
10 minutes

Part 2. Meditation Experience
'Gideon Experience'

Biblical Scripture

> And it was so: for he rose up early on the morrow and thrust the fleece together, and wringed the dew out of the fleece, a bowl full of water.
>
> JUDGES 6:38

Meditate on 10 discerning methods you can tell that something good is about to happen to you and give you

Happy and lovely feelings.

Goal II. Stimulate the Brain Cells

Part 1. Mental Health Challenge
40 minutes

Part 2. Recitation Experience
Name 25 animals in the wild

Goal III. Get the Body in Motion

Part 1`. Physical Mental Challenge
40 minutes

Part 2. Exercise Activity

'Imaginary Golf Swings' – Simulate Swinging motions with an imaginary golf club for 200 times on the left side and 200 times on the right side.

SHOUT HALLELUJAH!

Hints 25 wild animals

1. Coyotes
2. Grey wolves
3. Bobcats
4. Bears
5. Panthers
6. Rabbits
7. Squirrels
8. Raccoons
9. Rats

10. Snakes
11. Opossums
12. Armadillos
13. Deer
14. Lizards
15. Gophers
16. Wild Horses
17. Wild Hogs
18. Wild Turkeys
19. Wild Ducks
20. Wild Geese
21. Antelopes
22. Foxes
23. Mountain Lions
24. Egrets
25. Owls

CHAPTER 32

FEEL GOOD WORD OF THE DAY: ACCOMPLISHMENTS

On the Thirtieth- Second (32) Day of the Solo-Quarantine Experience - Celebrate Accomplishments

Def something that has been achieved successfully

Goal I: Gain Peace and Gratitude

Part 1. Spiritual Health Happy
And Love Challenge
10 minutes

Part 2. Meditation Experience
'Predicting the Future Experience'

Biblical Scripture

> Where there is no vision, the people perish, but he that keepth the law, happy is he.
>
> PROVERBS 29:18

Meditate on 10 past experiences that bought you happiness and love that came true that were once future experiences.

Goal II: Stimulate the Brain Cells

Part 1. Mental Health Challenge
40 minutes

Part 2. Recitation Experience
Name 25 common brand names.

Goal III: Get the Body in Motion

Part 1. Physical Health Challenge
40 minutes

Part 2. Exercise Activity
'Picking up the Pennies' - Do not bend knees -Spread 100 pennies or change around the room and pick them up one at
A time for 40 minutes

SHOUT HALLELUJAH!

Hints -Common Brand Names

1. Kraft
2. Hunts
3. Campbells
4. Libbys
5. Johnson and Johnson
6. Birdseyes
7. Hotpoint
8. Kenmore
9. Sara Lees
10. Idaho Potatoes
11. Kelloggs

12. Posts
13. French's
14. Hellmans
15. Liptons
16. Kool Aid
17. Sun Maid
18. Band Aid
19. Nyquill
20. Coca Cola
21. Pepsi
22. Dr. Pepper
23. Sun Kist
24. Keeblers
25. Nabisco

CHAPTER 33

FEEL -GOOD WORD OF THE DAY: WINNER

On the Thirtieth -third (33) Day of the Solo-Quarantine Experience Celebrate Winner

Def one that is successful especially through praiseworthy ability and hard work, a victor

Goal I: Gain Peace and Gratitude

Part 1. Spiritual Health Happy and Love
Connected Challenge
10 minutes

Part 2. Meditation Experience
'Finding Light Experience'

Biblical Scripture

> The Lord is my light and my salvation; whom shall I fear? The Lord is the strength of my life: of whom shall I be afraid?
>
> PSALM 27:1

Meditate 10 fears you have overcome and gained a sense of happiness and love

Goal II. Stimulate Brain Cells

Part 1. Mental Health Challenge
40 minutes

Part 2. Recitation Experience
Name 25 different types of spices, herbs and flavors

Goal III. Get the Body in Motion

Part 1. Physical Health Challenge
40 Minutes

Part 2. Exercise Activity

SHOUT HALLELUJAH!

Hints – Types of spices, herbs and flavors

1. Allspice
2. Nutmeg
3. Cayenne
4. Cinnamon
5. Cumin
6. Thyme
7. Rosemary
8. Sesame
9. Black pepper
10. Ginger
11. Cloves
12. Mace
13. Fennel
14. Mace

15. Cardamon
16. Curry
17. Cloves
18. Turmeric
19. Saffron
20. Bay leaves
21. Paprika
22. Vanilla Beans
23. Almond Extract
24. Peppermint Extract
25. Sage

CHAPTER 34

FEEL -GOOD WORD OF THE DAY: INDEPENDENCE

On the thirtieth-fourth (34) Day of the Solo-Quarantine Experience - Celebrate Independence

Def freedom from being ruled by a person or the ability to live your life freely

Goal I: Gain Peace and Gratitude

Part 1. Spiritual Health Happy and Love
Challenge
10 minutes

Part 2. Meditation Experience
'Flying like an Eagle Experience'

Biblical Scripture

> But they that wait upon the Lord shall renew their strength; they shall mount up with wings as eagles; they shall run, and not be weary; they shall walk, and not faint.
>
> ISAIAH 40:1

Meditate on 10 high achievements you have met and gained success.

Goal II: Stimulate Brain Cells

Part 1. Mental Health Challenge
40 minutes

Part 2. Recitation Experience
Name the keys on the piano

Goal III. Get the Body in Motion

Part 1. Physical Health Challenge
40 minutes

Part 2. Exercise Activity

SHOUT HALLELUJAH!

Hints – Keys on a piano
88 Keys on a piano
MIDDLE CDEFGABCDEFGABC

CHAPTER 35

FEEL- GOOD WORD OF THE DAY: SUPPORT

On the Thirtieth-Fifth(35) Day of the Solo-Quarantine Experience - Celebrate Support

Def to endure bravely or quietly

Goal I: Gain Peace and Gratitude

Part 1. Spiritual Health Happy and Love
Connected Challenge
10 minutes

Part 2. Meditation Experience
Brave Warrior Experience

Biblical Scripture

> The steps of a good man are ordered by the LORD: And he delighteth in his way.
>
> PSALM 37:23

Meditate on 10 brave steps you have taken to bring happiness and love.

Goal II: Stimulate Brain Cells

Part 1`. Mental Health Challenge
40 minutes

Part 2. Recitation Experience
Name 20 different television networks

Goal III. Get the Body in Motion

Part 1. Physical Health Challenge
40 minutes

Part 2. Exercise Activity

SHOUT HALLELUJAH!

Hints- Type of Television Networks

1. CBS
2. TBS
3. ABC
4. TNT
5. NBC
6. TBN
7. WGN
8. ION
9. KRAUT
10. CWS
11. ESPN
12. OWN
13. FOOD NETWORK
14. OXYGEN
15. BET
16. MSBNC
17. FOX

18. CMT
19. 700 CLUB
20. QVC
21. LIFETIME
22. DISNEY
23. IMPACT
24. C-SPAN
25. HISTORY

CHAPTER 36

FEEL- GOOD WORD OF THE DAY: PRAY

On the Thirty-Sixth (36) Day of the Solo-Quarantine Experience
Celebrate-Pray

Def to make a request to God or Jesus Christ

Goal I: Gain Peace and Gratitude

Part 1. Spiritual Health Happy and Love
Connected Challenge

Part 2. Meditation Experience
'Gethsemane Experience'

Biblical Scriptures

Garden of Gethsemane
The Will of God
O my Father what be possible let this up pass from me, nevertheless not as I will, but Jesus as thou will

36 Then cometh Jesus with them unto a place called Gethsemane, and saith unto the disciples, set ye here, while I go and pray yonder.

MATHEW 26: 36-46

Meditate on 10 ways you pray to get happiness and love.

Goal II: Stimulate Brain Cells

Part 1. Mental Health Challenge
40 minutes

Part 2. Recitation Experience
Recite the Lord's Prayer 25 times

Goal III: Get the Body in Motion

Part 1. Physical Health Challenge
40 minutes

Part 2. Exercise Activity

'Spring Frog Move' - Lie flat on your back on the mat or rug reach for the toes 100 times, while lying flat.
Use 40 minutes to do these exercises.

SHOUT HALLELUJAH!

Hint -The Lord's Prayer
Our Father who art in heaven,
Hallowed be thy Name,
Thy Kingdom come.
Thy will be done
On earth as it is in heaven.
Give us this day our daily bread.
And forgive us our debts,

As we forgive our debtors,
And lead us not into temptation,

But deliver as from evil

For thine is the Kingdom,
The power, and the glory, for ever.

Amen

MATTHEW 6:9-13

CHAPTER 37

FEEL -GOOD WORD OF THE DAY: CLOSURE

On the Thirtieth-Seventh (37) Day of the Solo-Quarantine Experience
Celebrate Closure

Def Process of shutdown or finishing up

Goal I: Gain Peace and Gratitude

Part 1: Spiritual Health Happy and Love Connected Challenge
10 minutes

Part 2. Meditation Experiences
'Jude Experience'

Biblical Scriptures

24 Now unto him that is able to keep you from falling, and to present you faultless before the presence of his glory with exceeding joy.

> 25 To the only wise God, our Saviour, be glory and majesty, dominion and, power, both now and ever, Amen.
>
> JUDE 1: 24,25

Meditate on 10 happenings somebody has given you to bring closure to bad situations in your life that that brought

Happiness and love in your life.

Goal II. Stimulate the Brain Cells

Part 1. Mental Health Challenge
40 minutes

Part 2. Recitation Experience
Name 25 types of Native American Tribes
(see Hints-Native American Tribes)

Goal III. Get the Body in Motion

Part 1. Physical Health Challenge
40 minutes

Part 2. Exercise Activity

'Knee -Slapping in Motions' -Sit up straight in your straight back chair, stretch out your hands parallel to your knees. Alternately bring each knee up to the stretched out hands 100 times.

SHOUT HALLELUJAH!

Hints –
Native American Tribes

1. Cherokees
2. Choctaws
3. Chickasaws
4. Creeks

5. Seminoles
6. Kickapoo
7. Osage
8. Caddo
9. Arapaho
10. Iowa
11. Ponca
12. Yuchi
13. Odawa
14. Cayuga
15. Tonkawa
16. Wichita
17. Waco
18. Apache
19. Coushatta
20. Modoc
21. Meshasaki
22. Pawnee
23. Waco
24. Commanche
25. Muscogee Creek
26. Sioux
27. Blackfoot
28. Shawnee
29. Kiowa
30. Cheyenne
31. Crow
32. Kaw

CHAPTER 38

FEEL- GOOD WORD OF THE DAY: ROYALTY

On the Thirty-Eighth (38) Day of the Solo-Quarantine Experience -Celebrate Royalty

Def treatment as an honor and a privilege

Goal I: Gain Peace and Gratitude

Part 1. Spiritual Health Happy and Love Challenge
10 minutes

Part 2. Meditation Experience
'Finding the truth of the Life Experience'
Queen of Sheba

Biblical Scripture

> And when the queen of Sheba heard of the fame of Solomon concerning the name of the LORD, she came to prove him with hard questions.
>
> I KINGS 10:1

Meditate on 10 wisdom experiences you have for happiness and love.

Goal II: Stimulate the Brain Cells

Part I. Mental Health Challenge
40 minutes

Part 2. Recitation Experience
Name 20 countries on the Asia continent
(see Hints on countries on the Asia continents)

Goal III. Get the Body in Motion

Part 1. Physical Health Challenge
40 minutes

Part 2. Exercise Activity

'Praying Mantis Moves' Using the mat or rug, get on your knees, using your hands for balance, bow from the waist and place the head to the floor 100 times.

SHOUT HALLELUJAH!

Hint – Countries on the Asia Continent

1. China
2. Korea
3. Philippines
4. Cambodia
5. Israel
6. India
7. Pakistan
8. Turkey
9. Iran
10. Yemen
11. Kuwait

12. Saudi Arabi
13. Afghanistan
14. Iraq
15. Lebanon
16. Palestine
17. Thailand
18. Korea
19. Mymmar
20. Japan
21. Cambodia
22. Taiwan

CHAPTER 39

FEEL - GOOD WORD OF THE DAY: PETS OR ANIMALS

On the Thirty-Ninth (39) Day of the Solo-Quarantine Experience -Celebrate Pets or Animals

Goal I: Gain Peace and Gratitude

Part 1. Spiritual Health Happy and Love Connected Challenge
10 minutes

Part 2. Meditation Experiences
'Animals friends to man Experience;

Biblical Scripture

> By faith Noah, being warned of God of things not seen as yet, moved with fear, prepared an ark to the saving of his house; By the which condemned the world, and became heir of the Righteousness which is by faith.
>
> HEBREW 11:7

Meditate on 10 ways a pet or animal has made you happy and in love.

Goal II: Stimulate Brain Cells

Part 1. Mental Health Challenge
40 minutes

Part 2. Recitation Experience
Name 50 pairs of animals on Noah's Ark
(See Hints-Animals on the Noah's Ark)

Goal III. Get the Body in Motion

Part 1. Physical Health Challenge
40 minutes

Part 2. Exercise Activity
Doggie Walk – Walk on your tip toes for 40 minutes without rest

SHOUT HALLELUJAH!

(see Hints)
A List of some of the animals that were on Noah's Ark

1. Elephants
2. Monkeys
3. Moose
4. Zebras
5. Hippos
6. Sheep
7. Cows
8. Giraffes
9. Bison
10. Bear
11. Kangaroos
12. Donkeys
13. Horses
14. Lions

15. Hogs
16. Walrus
17. Rabbits
18. Emus
19. Zebras
20. Frogs
21. Birds
22. Doves
23. Crows
24. Frogs
25. Turtles
26. Skunks
27. Lizards
28. Badgers
29. Ravens
30. Penguins

CHAPTER 40

FEEL -GOOD WORD OF THE DAY: TOUGH

On the Fortieth (40) Day of the Solo-Quarantine Experience -Celebrate Tough

Def Strong, firm and resilient

Goal I: Gain Peace and Gratitude

Part 1. Spiritual Health Happy and Love Connected Challenge
10 minutes

Part 2. Meditation Experience
'Trusting Experiences'

Biblical Scriptures

> 5Trust in the Lord with all thine heart, and lean not unto thine own understanding
>
> 1 In all thy ways acknowledge him, and he shall direct thy paths.
>
> PROVERBS 3:5,6

Meditate on 10 supernatural occasions you have achieved that have brought you happiness and love.

Goal II. Stimulate Brain Cell

Part 1. Mental Health Challenge
40 minutes

Part 2. Recitation Experiences
Name 25 types of insects
(see Hints – Types of Insects)

Goal III: Get the Body in Motion

Part 1. Physical Health Challenge
40 minutes

Part 2. Exercise Activity

'Guinea Fowl Stance' - Simulated Hand Stands -try holding on to the back of the straight back chair. Lower head to the seat of the chair and kick left leg straight out on the right and turn and quick left leg straight out to the left.

SHOUT HALLELUJAH!

Hints -Types of Insects

1. Mosquito
2. Roach
3. Gnats
4. Ants
5. Ladybug
6. Butterfly
7. Worm
8. Flies
9. Grasshopper

10. Spider
11. Dragonfly
12. Praying mantis
13. Bumble bee
14. Wasp
15. Yellow jacket
16. Ticks
17. Honey bee
18. Crickets
19. Butterfly
20. Moths
21. Worms
22. Snails
23. Baits
24. Beetle bugs

CHAPTER 41

FEEL -GOOD WORD OF THE DAY: FAMILY

On the Forty-first (41) Day of the Solo-Quarantine Experience -Celebrate Family

Def the basic unit in society traditionally consisting of two parents rearing their children

Goal I: Gain Peace and Gratitude

Part I. Spiritual Health Happy and Love
Connected Challenge
10 minutes

Part II. Meditation Experience
Joseph's Experience -Family

Biblical Scriptures

> 2 Joseph brothers were jealous of his relationship with their father. The brothers told lies and tried to destroy him, but God step forward.

> 3 Now Israel loved Joseph more than all his children, because he was the son of his old age: and he made him a coat of many colors.
>
> 4 And when his brethren saw that more than all his brethren, they hated him, and could not speak peaceably unto him.
>
> 45:4 And Joseph said unto his brethren, come near to me, I pray you. And they came near, And he said, I am Joseph your brother, whom ye sold into Egypt.
>
> GENESIS 37:2-4; 45:4

Meditate 10 minutes on the meaning of family and think on ways your family make you feel happy and love.

Goal II: Stimulate the Brain Cells

Part 1. Mental Health Challenge
40 minutes

Part 2. Recitation Experience
Name 1st, 2nd and 3rd Generation on both mother and father relatives (This is up to you!)
(see Hints)

Goal III: Get the Body in Motion

Part 1. Physical Health Challenge
10 minutes

Part 2. Exercise Activity
'Paddling the Canoe Boat Motions' - Simulate rowing a canoe motion for 100 times for 40 minutes.

SHOUT HALLELUJAH!

Hints –

1. Your First Cousins
2. Your Second Cousins
3. Your Third Cousins

CHAPTER 42

FEEL -GOOD WORD OF THE DAY: MINDFUL

On the Forty-second (42) Day of the Solo -Quarantine Experience -Celebrate Mindful

Def conscious or aware of something

Goal I: Gain Peace and Gratitude

Part 1. Spiritual Health Happy and Love Connected Challenge
10 minutes

Part 2. Meditation Experience
Experience 'Mindful of the Past Blessings from the LORD'

Biblical Scripture

> When a man's ways please the LORD, he maketh even his enemies to be at peace with him.
>
> PROVERBS 16:7

Meditate on 10 items you are mindful of that give you feelings of happy and love.

Goal II: Stimulate the Brain Cells

Part 1. Mental Health Challenge
40 minutes

Part 2. Recitation Experience
Name 25 types of jellies and jams
(see Hints-Jellies and Jams)

Goal III: Get the Body in Motion

Part 1. Physical Health Challenge
40 minutes

Part 2. Exercise Activity
'Happy Jumps' – Jump two feet forward; jump two feet backward 25 times

SHOUT HALLELUJAH!

Hints-Jellies and Jams

1. Grape Jelly
2. Grape Jam
3. Apricot Jelly
4. Apricot Jam
5. Plum Jelly
6. Plum Jam
7. Fig Jam
8. Apple Jelly
9. Strawberry Jelly
10. Strawberry Jam
11. Peach Jelly
12. Pepper Jelly
13. Peach Jam
14. Blueberry Jelly

15. Blueberry Jam
16. Blackberry Jelly
17. Blackberry Jam
18. Dewberry Jelly
19. Dewberry Jam
20. Pear Jam
21. Pear Jelly
22. Guava Jelly
23. Guava Jam
24. Orange Jelly
25. Orange Marmalade

CHAPTER 43

FEEL -GOOD WORD OF THE DAY: REST

On the Forty- third (43) Day of the Solo-Quarantine Journey - Celebrate -Rest

Def a repose, sleep or minimal functional and metabolic activities.

Goal I: Gain Peace and Gratitude

Part 1. Spiritual Health Happy and Love Connected
Challenge
10 minutes

Part 2. Meditation Experience
Rest for the weary experience

Biblical Scripture

> "Keep thy heart with all diligence for out of it are the issues of life.
>
> PROVERBS 4:23

Goal II: Stimulate Brain Cells

Part 1 Mental Health Challenge
40 minutes

Part 2. Recitation Experiences
Name 20 colors of roses
(see Hints -Colors of Roses)

Goal III: Get the Body in Motion

Part 1. Physical Health Challenge
40 minutes

Part 2. Exercise Activity
'Belly Roll' -Roll your belly 100 times while standing on your toes.

SHOUT HALLELUJAH!

Hints -Color of Roses

1. White
2. Pink
3. Red
4. Purple
5. Yellow
6. Ivory
7. Peach
8. Orange
9. Green
10. Ruby Red
11. Beige
12. Grey
13. Silver
14. Light Pink
15. Gold Metallic

16. Violet
17. Off White
18. Hot Pink
19. Lavender
20. Fuchsia
21. Ruby Yellow
22. Beige
23. Blue
24. Light Yellow
25. Ruby Blue

CHAPTER 44

FEEL -GOOD WORD OF THE DAY: CHEERFULNESS

On the Forty-fourth (44) Day of the Solo-Quarantine Experience -Celebrate Cheerfulness

Def the quality or state of being happy and optimistic.

Goal I: Gain Patience and Gratitude

Part 1. Spiritual Health Happy and Love-Connected Challenge

Part 2 – Meditation Experience
'Good Heart Experience'

Biblical Scripture

> A merry heart doeth good like a medicine; But a broken spirit drieth the bones.
>
> PROVERBS 17:22

Meditate on 10 good practices to keep the heart healthy and happy.

Goal II: Stimulate Brain Cells

Part 1 Mental Health Challenge
40 minutes

Part 2 Recitation Experience
Name 20 types of bones in the body
(see Hints Bones in the Body)

Goal III Get the Body in Motion

Part I Physical Health Challenge
40 minutes

Part II. Exercise Activity

'Wild Ducks Flapping' - Simulate wild ducks flying south, by stretching your arms and flapping in circular motions 100 times.

SHOUT HALLELUJAH!

Hints – Names of 20 bones in the body.
There are 206 bones in the body

1. Cranium
2. Mandible
3. Maxilla
4. Clavicle
5. Scapala
6. Humerus
7. Radius
8. Ulna
9. Carpals
10. Metacarpals
11. Phalanges
12. Sternum
13. Ribs

14. Cervical
15. Thoracic
16. Sacrum
17. Lumbar
18. Coccyx
19. Femur
20. Patella
21. Fibula
22. Talus
23. Tibia
24. Sternum
25. Ribs

CHAPTER 45

FEEL -GOOD WORD OF THE DAY: CONSCIENCE

On the Forty-fifth (45) Day of the Solo-Quarantine Experience -Celebrate Conscience

Def an inner feeling or voice viewed as acting as a guide to the rightness or wrongness of one's behavior.

Goal I: Gain Peace and Gratitude

Part 1. Spiritual Health Happy and Love -Connected Challenge
10 minutes

Part 2. Meditation Experience
'Good Conscience Experience'

Biblical Scripture

> What shall we then say to these things? If God be for us, who can be against us?
>
> ROMANS 8:31

Meditate on 10 measures that bring about good conscience decisions.

Goal II: Stimulate the Brain Cells

Part 1 Mental Health Challenge
40 minutes

Part 2 Recitation Challenge
Name 20 different types of teachers
(see Hints for Teachers classifications)

Goal III: Get the Body in Motion

Part 1 Physical Health Challenge
40 minutes

Part 2 Exercise Activity
'Leg Elevation Challenge'- Sit in the chair and raise straighten out the legs and bring both legs to the sky for 25 times

SHOUT HALLELUJAH!

Hints -Teachers Classifications

1. Elementary science
2. Elementary gym
3. Elementary math
4. Junior High earth science
5. Junior High chemistry
6. Senior High language arts
7. Arts teacher
8. Physical education teacher
9. Special education teacher
10. Biology teacher
11. Family and Consumer Sciences Teacher
12. Agriculture teachers
13. Industrial arts teacher
14. Music Teacher

15. Spanish teacher
16. French teacher
17. Library Teacher
18. Computer Science Teacher
19. Social Science teacher
20. Earth Science Teacher
21. General Math Teacher
22. Geometry Teacher
23. Advanced Science Teacher
24. Advanced Math Teacher
25. English Literature Teacher
26. History Teachers

CHAPTER 46

FEEL GOOD WORD OF THE DAY: AGREEMENT

On the Forty-sixth (46) Day of the Solo-Quarantine Experience-Celebrate -Agreement

Def harmony of opinion, action or character in a transaction

Goal I: Gain Peace and Gratitude

Part 1. Spiritual Health Happy and Love-Connected Challenge
10 minutes

Part 2. Meditation Experience
'The duties of the elderly experiences'

Biblical Experiences

2 That the aged men be sober, grave, temperate, sound in faith, in charity, in patience

3 The aged women likewise that they be in behaviour as becometh holiness, not false accusers, not given to much wine, teachers of good things:

4 That they may teach the young women to be sober, to have their husbands, to love their children.

5 To be discreet, chaste, keepers at home, good, obedient to their own husbands, that the word obedient to their own husbands, that the word of God be not blasphemed

6 Young men likewise exhort to be sober minded.

2 In all things showing thyself a pattern of good works: in doctrine showing uncorruptness, gravity, sincerity,

3 Sound speech, that cannot be condemned: that he that is of the contrary part may be ashamed, having no evil thing to say of you.

TITUS 2:2-8

Meditate on 10 good decisions you have given young people to make them prosperous.

Goal II: Stimulate Brain Cells

Part 1. Mental Health Challenge
40 minutes

Part 2. Recitation Experience
Name 25 types of Fish
(see Hints -Types of Fish)

Goal III: Get the Body in Motion

Part 1. Physical Health Challenge
40 minutes

Part 2. Exercise Activity
Neck Rolls- Roll your Neck from left to right for 50 times.

SHOUT HALLELUJAH!

Hints -Types of Fish

1. Bass
2. Catfish
3. Perch
4. Salmon
5. Flounder
6. Shark
7. Whale
8. Carp
9. Shrimp
10. Lobster
11. Clam
12. Oysters
13. Halibut
14. Trout
15. Mackerel
16. Tuna
17. Tilapia
18. Gold fish
19. Piranha
20. Stingray
21. Cod
22. Sole
23. Mahi Mahi
24. Logostino
25. Hogfish

CHAPTER 47

FEEL GOOD WORD OF THE DAY: CHALLENGE

On the Forty-seventh (47) Day of the Solo-Quarantine Experience -Celebrate Challenge

Def a call to take part in a contest or competition

Goal I: Gain Peace and Gratitude

Part 1. Spiritual Health Happy and Love Connected Challenge 10 minutes

Part 2 Meditation Experience

Biblical Scripture

> Every good gift and every perfect gift is from above, and cometh down from the Father of lights, with whom is no variableness, neither shadow of turning.
>
> JAMES 1:17

Meditate on 10 challenges that made you happy and good loe.

Goal II: Stimulate Brain Cells

Part 1. Mental Health Challenge
40 minutes

Part 2. Recitation Experience
Name the countries on the North America Continent
(see Hint -North American Countries)

Goal III: Get the Body in Motion

Part 1. Physical Health Challenge
40 minutes

Part 2. Exercise Activity

The Miracle Dance -Dance from side to side 10 times -then jump up high at least 10 inches for 20 times

SHOUT HALLELUJAH!

Hints -North American Countries

1. United States
2. Canada
3. Mexico
4. Bahamas
5. Jamaica
6. Antigua
7. Barbados
8. Belize
9. Costa Rica
10. Dominica
11. Dominican Republic
12. Greenland
13. Panama
14. Nevis and Saint Lucia

15. Saint Vincent and Grenadines
16. Saint Maartin
17. Dominica
18. Trinidad and Tobago
19. Honduras
20. Iceland
21. Haiti
22. Cuba
23. St. John
24. St. Croix
25. St. Vincent

CHAPTER 48

FEEL- GOOD WORD OF THE DAY: DREAMS

On the Forty-eighth (48) Day of the Solo-Quarantine Experience Celebrate Dreams

Def. happenings during sleep

Goal I: Gain Peace and Gratitude

Part 1. Spiritual Health Happy and Love-Connected Challenge
10 minutes

Part 2. Meditation Experience
Covenant Experience

Biblical Scripture

> 12 And God said, this is the token of the covenant which I made between me and you and every being creative that is with you, for perpetual generations.

> 13 I do set my bow in the cloud, and it shall be for a token
> of in covenant between me and the earth.
>
> GENESIS 8:12, 13

Meditate on 10 dreams you remember that came true and made you feel happy and love.

Goal II: Stimulate the Brain Cells

Part 1. Mental Health Challenge
40 minutes

Part 2. Recitation Experience
Name the 25 countries on the European continent
(see Hints -European Countries)

Goal III: Get the Body in Motion

Part 1. Physical Health Challenge
40 minutes

Part 2. Exercise Activity
Shoot for the Stars Motions- Make 25 jumps while pointing both point fingers toward the sky.

SHOUT HALLELUJAH!

Hints – 25 European Countries

1. England
2. Wales
3. Germany
4. Italy
5. Sweden
6. Greece

7. Poland
8. Finland
9. Belgium
10. 10.The Netherlands
11. Latvia
12. Lithuania
13. Luxemburg
14. Malta
15. Portugal
16. Romania
17. Slovakia
18. Slovenia
19. Spain
20. Austria
21. Scotland
22. Norway
23. Bulgaria
24. Czech Republic
25. Estonia
26. Cyprus

CHAPTER 49

FEEL GOOD WORD OF THE DAY: AWARD

On the Forty-ninth (49) Day of the Solo-Quarantine Experience-Celebrate- Award

Def to confer or bestow as being deserved or merited or needed.

Goal 1: Gain Patience and Gratitude

Part 1 Spiritual Health Happy and Love
Connected Challenge
10 minutes

Part 2. Meditation Experience
Meaning of the Twelve Stones

Biblical Scriptures

19 And the people came out of Jordan on the tenth day of the first month, and encamped in Gilgal, in the east border of Jericho

20 And those twelve stones, which they took out of Jordan, did Joshua pitch in Gilgal.

21 And he spake unto the children of Israel, saying, when your children shall ask their fathers in times to come, saying what mean these stones?

22 Then ye shall let your children know, saying. Israel came over this Jordan on dry land.

23 For the LORD your God dried up the waters of Jordan from before you, until ye were passed over, us LORD your God did to the Red Sea, where he dried up from before us, until we were gone over.

24 That all the people of the earth might know the hand of the LORD, that it is mighty: That ye might fear the LORD your God for ever.

JOSHUA 4:19-24

Meditate on 10 traditions handed down in your family that have brought you happiness and love.

Goal II: Stimulate the Brain Cells

Part 1. Mental Health Challenge
40 minutes

Part 2. Recitation Experience
Name the 66 books of the Holy Bible
(see Hints-Books of the Bible)

Goal III: Get the Body in Motion

Part 1. Physical Health Challenge
40 minutes

Part 2. Exercise Experience

'Hip -Hip -Up in the Air' - Lie on the floor stretch out - Raise let hip up in the air while lying on the right side 25 times and turn and lie on the left side and raise the left hip up for 25 times.

SHOUT HALLELUJAH!

Hints -Book in the Bible

OLD AND NEW TESTAMENTS OF THE HOLY BIBLE

1. Acts
2. Amos
3. I Chronicles
4. II Chronicles
5. Colossians
6. I Corinthians
7. II Corinthians
8. Daniel
9. Deuteronomy
10. Ecclesiastes
11. Ephesians
12. Esther
13. Exodus
14. Ezekiel
15. Ezra
16. Galatians
17. Genesis
18. Habakkuk
19. Haggai
20. Hebrews
21. Hosea
22. Isaiah
23. James
24. Jeremiah
25. Job
26. Joel

27. John
28. I John
29. 2 John
30. 3 John
31. Jonah
32. Joshua
33. Jude
34. Judges
35. I Kings
36. 2 Kings
37. Lamentations
38. Leviticus
39. Luke
40. Malachi
41. Mark
42. Matthew
43. Micah
44. Nahum
45. Nehemiah
46. Numbers
47. Obadiah
48. I Peter
49. II Peter
50. Philemon
51. Philippians
52. Proverbs
53. Psalms
54. Revelations
55. Romans
56. Ruth
57. I Samuel
58. 2 Samuel
59. Song of Solomon
60. 1 Thessalonians
61. 2 Thessalonians
62. 1 Timothy

63. 2 Timothy
64. Titus
65. Zechariah
66. Zephaniah

CHAPTER 50

FEEL GOOD WORD OF THE DAY: PROVISION

On the Fiftieth (50) Day of the Solo -Quarantine Experience - Celebrate Provision

Def the action of providing or supplying something for use -equipping, giving

Goal I: Gain Peace and Gratitude

Part 1. Spiritual Health Happy and
And Love -Connected Challenge
10 minutes

Part 2. Meditation Experience

Biblical Scripture

> A good name is rather to be chosen that great riches, and loving favour rather than silver and gold.
>
> PROVERBS 22:1

Meditate on 10 experience you have had that were caused due to your good name.

Goal II: Stimulate the Brain Cells

Part 1. Mental Health Challenge
40 minutes

Part 2. Recitation Experience
Name 25 common last names
(see Hints Common Last Names)

Goal III: Get the Body in Motion

Part 1. Physical Health Challenge
40 minutes

Part 2. Exercise Activity
Horse Prancing – Prance in place, similar to a horse, for 40 minutes.

SHOUT HALLELUJAH!

Hints- Common Last Names

1. Smith
2. Jones
3. Jackson
4. Washington
5. Greens
6. Blues
7. Browns
8. Johnson
9. Lowes
10. Whites
11. Coopers
12. Anderson

13. Reed
14. Williams
15. Johnston
16. Fords
17. Banks
18. Littles
19. Lemons
20. Blacks
21. Murphy
22. Myles
23. Murray
24. Birds
25. Cannons

CHAPTER 51

FEEL GOOD WORD OF THE DAY: HARD WORK

On the Fifty-first (51) Day of the Solo-Quarantine Experience -Celebrate Hard work

Constantly regularly, or habitually engaged in earnest and energetic work: industrious, diligent

Goal I: Gain Patience and Gratitude

Part 1. Spiritual Health Happy and Love Connected Challenge
10 minutes

Part 2. Meditation Experience
Ruth Experience

Biblical Scripture

> And Boaz said unto her, At mealtime come thou hither, and at -of the bread, and dip thy morsel in the vinegar. And she sat beside the reapers. And hereseted her parched corn, and she did eat, and was sufficed, and left.
>
> RUTH 3:24

Meditate on 10 examples of how results of hard work has brought you feelings of happiness and love.

Goal II: Stimulate the Brain Cells

Part 1. Mental Health Challenge
40 minutes

Part 2. Recitation Experience
Name 25 Furry Animals
(see Hints -Furry Animals)

Goal III. Get the Body in Motion

Part 1. Physical Health Challenge
40 minutes

Part 2. Exercise Activity

'Tree Hugging Activity' - Simulate hugging a large tree three feet in diameter repeatedly for 100 times f0r 40 minutes

SHOUT HALLELUJAH!

Hints -Furry Animals

1. Dogs
2. Cats
3. Horses
4. Donkeys
5. Tigers
6. Lions
7. Monkeys
8. Skunks
9. Raccoons
10. Opossums

11. Mules
12. Rats
13. Squirrels
14. Bears
15. Bobcats
16. Links
17. Slugs
18. Cheetah
19. rabbits
20. gopher
21. ground hog
22. pigs
23. cows
24. giraffe
25. camel
26. (people's hair)

Notes to the Solo -Quarantine People:

1. Evaluate your daily progress.
2. Create your personal challenges!

REFERENCES

1. Holy Bible King James Version, Gideon International, Nashville, Tenn. National Publishing Company, 1978.

Printed in the United States
by Baker & Taylor Publisher Services